04

0 0001 6721994 8

PLAZA

D1367615

Transportation & Communication Series

The U.S. Mail

Elaine A. Kule

Enslow Publishers, Inc.

40 Industrial Road	PO Box 38
Box 398	Aldershot
Berkeley Heights, NJ 07922	Hants GU12 6BP
USA	UK

http://www.enslow.com

To Sophie and Oscar,
who I know will enjoy receiving mail as much as I do.

Copyright © 2002 by Enslow Publishers, Inc.

All rights reserved.

No part of this book may be reproduced by any means without the written permission of the publisher.

Library of Congress Cataloging-in-Publication Data

Kule, Elaine A.
   The U.S. mail / Elaine A. Kule.
      p. cm. — (Transportation & communication series)
   Includes bibliographical references and index.
   Summary: Discusses the history of the United States mail from the Pony
Express to today and describes the mailing process.
   ISBN 0-7660-1892-X
   1. Postal service—United States—History—Juvenile literature. 2. Pony express—History—Juvenile
literature. [1. Postal service—History.] I. Title: United States mail. II. Title. III. Series.
   HE6371 .K85 2002
   383'.4973—dc21
                                      2001004011

Printed in the United States of America

10 9 8 7 6 5 4 3 2 1

To Our Readers:
We have done our best to make sure all Internet Addresses in this book were active and appropriate when we went to press. However, the author and the publisher have no control over and assume no liability for the material available on those Internet sites or on other Web sites they may link to. Any comments or suggestions can be sent by e-mail to comments@enslow.com or to the address on the back cover.

Every effort has been made to locate all copyright holders of material used in this book. If any errors or omissions have occurred, corrections will be made in future editions of this book.

Illustration Credits: Noah Addis/The Star Ledger, p. 37 (middle); AP Photo/Bob Daugherty, pp. 42, 43; The Bancroft Library, p. 8 (top); Frank Conlon/The Star Ledger, p. 18; Corel Corporation, pp. 6 (top), 10 (bottom), 39; Denver Public Library, Western History Collection, pp. 4, 6 (bottom), 7, 9, 10 (top), 11, 20; Dover Publications, Inc., pp. 29, 32, 34; Enslow Publishers, Inc., p. 44; Hemera Technologies, Inc. 1997-2000, pp. 1, 2, 5, 8, 13, 16 (top), 19, 21, 22, 23, 27, 33, 39, 40, 41; Tony Kurdzuk/The Star Ledger, p. 14; Library of Congress, pp. 12, 28, 30, 31, 35, 36, 37 (top and bottom); National Archives, pp. 24, 25, 26; Patti Sapone/The Star Ledger, p. 15; Star Ledger photo by Tom Kitts, p. 17; United States Postal Service Web site, <http://www.usps.gov>, p. 38; Star Ledger photo by Warren S. Westura, p. 16; Vic Yepello/The Star Ledger, p. 19 (bottom).

Cover Illustration: Enslow Publishers, Inc.; Flag image from PhotoDisc, Inc.

Contents

Chapter 1

The Pony Express

In 1860, people really had to wait to get their mail. Stagecoaches carrying letters from the East rode through the southern United States to reach California. The trip took more than twenty days.

An American businessman, William H. Russell, knew he could shorten the time. He decided to hire fast horseback riders to travel through the central United States. Russell and his partners, Alexander Majors and William B. Waddell, called their new mail service the Pony Express.

Russell bought strong horses. He put an

Before the Pony Express, stagecoaches carried mail from the East to the West (top left). Some stations looked like this (bottom left).

Riding a horse for the Pony Express was a dangerous job.

advertisement in newspapers for good horseback riders. The ad read: "Wanted: Young, skinny, wiry fellows not over 18. Must be expert riders willing to risk death daily. Orphans preferred."

On April 3, 1860, a crowd watched the first Pony Express rider take off in St. Joseph, Missouri. People cheered and waved flags. A band played lively music. The rider was one of about thirty other young men who would make the important trip over the next ten days.

For $25 a week, their job was to ride as fast as they could from St. Joseph to Sacramento, California— a distance of

1,966 miles. They faced robbers, bad weather, and bad trails to deliver the mail.

One Pony Express rider was Robert Haslam, who was later called Pony Bob. His route was a seventy-seven-mile trail in Nevada. Like the other riders, he would travel for ten or fifteen miles until he reached a Pony Express station. He had just two minutes to sip water or coffee and gulp the food the station worker gave him. Then he jumped on a rested horse and went on with his trip. After riding seventy-five to one hundred miles, Pony Bob stopped at a home station. He gave the mail to a waiting rider. Then he ate and slept. This was usually the end of his day. He had been riding for about eight hours.

But in May 1860, fighting broke out along Pony Bob's route. Native Americans thought that miners were taking their land. When Pony Bob rode to a station in Carson,

Robert Haslam was a Pony Express rider. He was called Pony Bob.

Pony Express riders would ride for ten or fifteen miles before stopping at a station like this one to eat and get rested horses (far left).

7

MAP OF THE
PONY EXPRESS TRAIL
FROM St. JOSEPH Mo. To SACRAMENTO CALIF.

Sacramento

St. Joseph

The first Pony Express rider took off from St. Joseph, Missouri, on his way to Sacramento, California.

Nevada, the horses were gone. The miners who were chasing the Native Americans had taken them.

Pony Bob let his horse rest. Then he went to the next station, where he planned to give the mail to another rider. But that man heard about the fighting and was afraid to leave.

Pony Bob went on. He came to a station that was burned to the ground. The worker

Before the United States Postal Service, there were small companies that delivered mail.

This is an old Pony Express station and its stables in Wyoming (top).

This is a marker showing where a Pony Express station once stood.

was dead and there were no horses. Pony Bob kept going. When there was no rider at the next stop, Pony Bob finished the route. In thirty-six hours, he had ridden 384 miles. It was the longest distance a Pony Express rider ever traveled in that amount of time.

At $5 for a half-ounce, the Pony Express cost too much for most people. The government and newspaper publishers were the service's biggest customers. The Pony Express also cost a lot to run. There were many people to pay and many horses to feed.

In 1861, the Pony Express lowered its rate from $5 a half-ounce to $1. After that, Russell and his partners lost many thousands of dollars.

On October 24, 1861, workers finished laying the telegraph lines connecting the East and West of the United States. A telegraph could send signals through wires and electric current. People could send messages faster and for less money than the Pony Express.

By then, the Pony Express had run out of money. It closed on October 26, 1861, but it earned a lasting place in America's history.

The Overland Mail Company not only delivered mail, but also gave people a way to travel.

Chapter 2

The Mail Trail

The U.S. mail has changed a lot since the Pony Express days. With the right amount of stamps and the right address, a letter can go to almost any place in the world.

Getting and sending mail in the United States is fast and easy. Letters are brought to homes and businesses five or six days a week, even in bad weather.

Letters are picked up one or more times a day, except on Sunday and national holidays. Pick-up times are listed on signs outside a mailbox or inside a slot's door. Most people are near some kind of mail collection box.

This photo from the 1900s shows a woman mailing a letter (left).

Mail going to the same city or town it is sent from usually arrives the next day. Delivery may take two or three days for letters going longer distances.

Here is what happens after an envelope slides down a mailbox. The letter falls into a plastic tub that sits at the bottom of the mailbox. A postal truck driver picks up the tub at a set time. Some drivers pour the mail from the tubs into large cloth bags. The letters go onto a truck and to the nearest post office that gets mail ready for processing.

Workers feed the mail into a machine called an Advanced Facer-Canceler System. This machine arranges letters so that each address faces the same way. Then it cancels and postmarks the stamped mail. Canceled stamps have wavy lines to show that they have been used once and cannot be used again. The

This letter carrier puts mail into mail boxes.

postmark shows the date and the city and state where the stamps were canceled.

The Advanced Facer-Canceler System sorts the mail into three groups: mail that has a handwritten address, mail that has an address printed by a typewriter or other machine, and mail that has a bar code. A bar code is a row of lines that has been sprayed on the envelope with an ink jet. The lines have ZIP Code information that is used to sort the mail for delivery. Bar codes are near the edge of an envelope.

Pictures of handwritten addresses are taken by the Advanced Facer-Canceler System. It sends the pictures to the Remote Bar Coding System. This machine reads the addresses from the pictures. Then it sprays a bar code on each envelope.

Mail that has an address printed by machine is sent to a Multiline Optical Character Reader. It reads the address and sprays a bar code on each envelope.

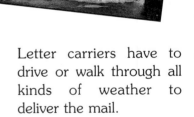

Letter carriers have to drive or walk through all kinds of weather to deliver the mail.

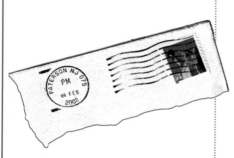

Postmarks and canceled stamps look like this.

People at the post office sort the mail.

Envelopes that have addresses that cannot be read are sent to the Remote Bar Coding System. Mail that cannot be read by machine is given to workers. They try to match the address on an envelope with a real address. If a match is found, the right bar code gets sprayed on the envelope.

Mail going to the same city is put in one section of the post office. Mail going further is put in other areas. The envelopes go into metal boxes.

Drivers put some boxes on trucks and drive to post offices that are close by. Other boxes will go on trucks to cities that are less than 200 miles away. Postal drivers will ride to the processing center that is closest to where the mail is going.

Mail going longer distances is taken to airports on trucks. The metal boxes are stored in the baggage section of airplanes that people use every day.

After the airplane lands, postal truck drivers take the metal boxes to a processing center that is closest to where the mail is going.

Postal workers unload the boxes at the post office. Letters are put in a sorting machine called the Delivery Bar Code System. It reads the bar codes of every letter. It also groups mail for each carrier's route. A route in a town or city is about five or six blocks long.

The mail is put in a carrier's bag, ready for

Some letter carriers walk on their mail routes.

Many cities and towns have post offices.

delivery. Vans or carts help the letter carriers on their routes. Some letter carriers only walk on their route.

Some addresses cannot be read by postal workers. Other envelopes do not have addresses at all. They are sent to one of the three Mail Recovery Centers in the United States. Workers there will open the mail to find out where it should go. If information from the letters is not found, the letters are kept for ninety days. After that, they are destroyed.

Writing or typing the correct name and address on an envelope helps a letter reach the right place quickly. The correct ZIP Code is needed, too. The sender's address, called a return address, should also be added. If an address is wrong or the person a letter is addressed to has moved, the mail can be returned to the sender.

There are more than 38,000 post offices in the United States and 312,000 mail collection boxes. People can also buy stamps and mail letters at the hundreds of self-service centers and mobile vans throughout the country. Stamps can be bought on the Internet, too.

Long ago, people had to wait months to hear from friends or family who lived far away. It took a lot of hard work and many people to get the postal service the way it is today.

Post offices are busy places.

Chapter 3

The Mail in Colonial Times

In ancient times, people in the Far East used runners to send messages to one another. The word "post" slowly came to mean "messages." Many people think "post" comes from the Latin word *ponere*, which means "to place."

There were no post offices in the early days of what is now the United States. During the 1600s, people asked friends and storeowners to deliver letters and messages within the thirteen colonies. British kings and their helpers ruled the colonies.

Many colonists came from England and

People in colonial times would bring their letters to storeowners. Travelers would then deliver the letters.

21

Travelers who were going to Europe would deliver letters.

other countries in Europe. They asked boat travelers to deliver letters to friends and family who lived far away.

The first postal service began in 1639 in Boston, Massachusetts. Government leaders let Richard Fairbanks use his tavern to collect mail going to and from Europe. Travelers left letters for people to pick up or for others to get them. People called post riders carried mail on routes called post roads. They picked up mail and left it with Fairbanks. He was allowed to charge one penny for handling each letter.

In 1692, King William III of England let Thomas Neale run the mail in the American colonies. Neale chose Governor Andrew Hamilton of New Jersey as Deputy Postmaster General. Hamilton set up the colonies' first postal system.

Envelopes and postage stamps were not used then. People folded their papers and wrote the names and addresses of the people they were going to on the outside. The people who received the letters paid the postage. The further the letter went and the heavier it was, the more money it cost.

The mail did not usually go to people's homes. People had to visit the post office and ask if they had mail. If people did not pick up their mail, it stayed at the post office. The postage costs were unpaid. The service was losing money.

In 1707, the British government decided to run the colonies' mail service. The main office was in the harbor city of New York. Letters going to England were packed and put on ships. Other post offices were built in New Hampshire, Pennsylvania, and Virginia.

Benjamin Franklin, a young printer and publisher, was chosen Postmaster of Philadelphia in 1737. A postmaster runs a post office.

In 1753, Franklin became Deputy Postmaster General of all thirteen colonies.

In 1753, Benjamin Franklin became Deputy Postmaster General of all thirteen colonies.

A postmaster general is in charge of all the post offices and its workers.

Franklin visited the post offices to make sure they were running well. He had the post roads cleared for mail delivery. Franklin also set times when the mail would be picked up. Beginning in 1756, stagecoaches were used for carrying mail between Philadelphia and New York. Later, Franklin started a twenty-four-hour service between the two cities and Boston.

Postal service in the colonies was getting better. But the rates were high. Many people decided not to use the royal postal system. They sent letters using secret carriers instead.

By 1774, the colonists wanted their freedom from British rule and King George III. Franklin was let go from his job for siding with the other colonists. William Goddard, a printer and publisher, set up a colonial mail service called the Constitutional Post.

In April 1775, fighting broke out between

colonists in Lexington, Massachusetts, and the British soldiers stationed there. The American Revolution had begun.

A group of colonists met in Philadelphia to plan a new government. The meeting was called the Second Continental Congress. One of the problems they talked about was mail delivery.

On July 26, 1775, the Congress picked Benjamin Franklin as Postmaster General of the thirteen colonies. He kept the job until November 1776.

Many of the practices Franklin started are still used. The Dead Letter Department, now called Mail Recovery, is one example.

The American Revolution started with the Battle of Lexington in April 1775.

Franklin made mail delivery better and faster. But he would surely be surprised at the many changes that happened over the years.

Sails, Rails, and Other Changes

By 1783, the American Revolution was over. After a long fight, the United States won its freedom from England. In the Constitution of the United States, America's first leaders wrote that the national government would run the postal service.

The Post Office Department bought stagecoaches, or horse-drawn wagons, to carry the mail in 1785. Horses were changed every fifteen or twenty miles at rest stops called stages. As people moved west, so did mail delivery.

In 1789, there were about seventy-five post offices in the United States. But many places

The American Revolution was over in 1783. Here, George Washington (left), who led the Colonial Army, rides into New York.

By 1813, the Post Office Department started using steamboats to deliver the mail.

These men are unloading mail from a train in the 1940s.

were not near post offices or post roads. By 1813, the Post Office Department was using steamboats to carry the mail. These ships had sails and an engine to move them. The steamboats went along the Hudson River, the Great Lakes, and the Mississippi River.

In 1832, the Post Office Department had trains carry the mail in Pennsylvania. Eight years later, there were railway routes for mail in New York and Massachusetts.

Congress, the nation's lawmakers, passed a law on July 7, 1838. It said that all railroads in the United States were post routes. Mail was carried on trains and delivered by postal workers to a town's post office.

There were more changes from the Post Office Department. The government issued the first postage stamps in 1847. Before then, postal clerks wrote "Paid" on envelopes.

One of the first stamps had a

picture of George Washington, the first president of the United States. Another stamp had a picture of Benjamin Franklin.

Yet people did not have to use stamps to send mail. They could pay for a letter before mailing it at a post office. They could also hope that the person they wrote to would pay for the mail.

But if people did not pick up their mail at the post office, the postage did not get paid. The Post Office Department lost a lot of money. By 1855, all envelopes needed a postage stamp.

In 1858, mail collection boxes began to appear on the streets of large cities. Now people did not have to go to post offices to send letters.

Western Union, a large telegraph company, completed the nation's first transcontinental telegraph line in 1861. Americans could send messages quickly to each other. Yet mail was still important to them.

A picture of George Washington was on one of the first stamps.

1. DUTTON THE CRANE: DELIVERING THE MAIL AND DAILY PAPERS AT THE PENNSYLVANIA RAILWAY DEPOT, AT JERSEY CITY. 2. INTERIOR OF CAR: DISTRIBUTING MAIL.
3. THE CATCH. 4. "READY TO THROW OFF."

THE RAILWAY MAIL SERVICE.—METHODS OF DISTRIBUTING AND DELIVERING THE MAIL.

FROM SKETCHES BY A STAFF ARTIST.—SEE PAGE 122.

These pictures show the different stages of mail delivery by train during the 1800s.

The Post Office Department kept working to reach more people, and to have faster delivery.

In 1864, the first United States Railroad Post Office was set up. Postal workers sorted mail on special railroad cars as the trains traveled between cities. The workers threw bags of letters for the town's people onto the railroad station platform. As the train moved by, a machine called a catcher arm picked up mailbags for delivery. By using the catcher arm, a train did not have to slow down to pick up mail at each town.

The railroad made mail delivery faster, but it did not help people who lived far from the nearest town. It often took a day for them to get to and from the nearest post office. Some people did not pick up their mail for months.

A special-delivery service for sending and receiving packages began in 1885. It helped thousands of people who lived far from a post office. And another big change was just a few years away.

In 1864, the first United States Railroad Post Office was set up. Postal workers sorted mail on special railroad cars, like this one.

Chapter 5

Rural Free Delivery and Air Mail

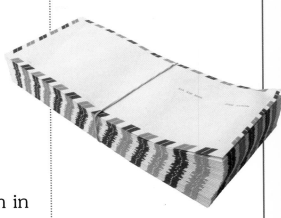

In 1896, Rural Free Delivery service began in West Virginia. Because the Post Office would only deliver to places that had good roads, other states worked to make their roads better. Mail carriers used horses and horse-drawn wagons called buggies to deliver the mail. They rode sleds on snow-covered ground in the winter.

In 1913, the Post Office Department started a package delivery service called Parcel Post. They also began Collect-On-Delivery, or COD, which let people pay for the things they bought when the packages were delivered to

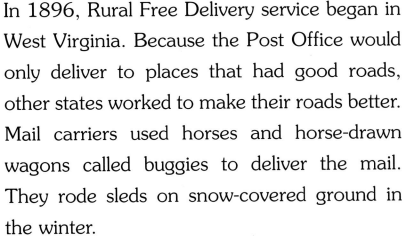

People could order items like clothes and have them delivered to their homes. These pages from a Sears mail order catalog show what boys and girls wore in the 1940s.

Orville and Wilbur Wright made the first engine-driven airplane in 1903.

their homes. The people who lived in these out-of-the-way places were happy. They ordered clothing, shoes, and other things through the mail. By 1915, Rural Free Delivery was a big success, covering over one million miles of the United States.

Rural Free Delivery helped unite the country. But the Post Office Department still wanted to speed mail delivery. They hoped the new airplanes could fly mail.

Orville and Wilbur Wright had made the first engine-driven flight in 1903. The brothers' work helped other people make airplanes stronger and faster.

In May 1918, airmail service started between New York and Washington, D.C. Pilots flew the open airplanes wearing leather masks, helmets, and flight suits. They needed protection from the strong, often icy winds.

Flying the early mail planes was a dangerous job. Pilots flew during bad weather. They did not have radios or other tools to help guide them while they were flying. There were no lights on the ground or in the airplane. There were few landing fields. Many pilots died in crashes.

Mail was carried on trains at night and on airplanes by day. But with better weather reporting through radios at each airfield, pilots could fly longer distances. In 1921, mail was flown day and night for the first time from San Francisco to New York.

Airmail service started in 1918.

Even though airmail helped deliver letters faster across the United States in the 1920s, letter carriers still had to deliver the mail to homes.

Congress gave the Post Office Department more money for airmail service. More landing fields were built. Towers and searchlights were set up. Airplanes had tools for guiding the planes and for nighttime flying.

But by 1925, Congress wanted to help build the airline business. The lawmakers asked the Post Office Department to work with the new airline companies and let them deliver mail.

In those early days, airmail within the United States cost more than first class mail, but the service was faster. Starting in 1975, nearly all first-class mail going more than 200 miles was put on airplanes. Two years later, mail flying within North America was no longer called airmail. It was grouped as first-class mail, just like other letters.

The United States Postal Service kept working to get mail to people quickly. Yet even more ways to bring people together lay ahead.

Post Offices come in all shapes and sizes.

U.S. airmail pilots might have been given pins like this one to wear.

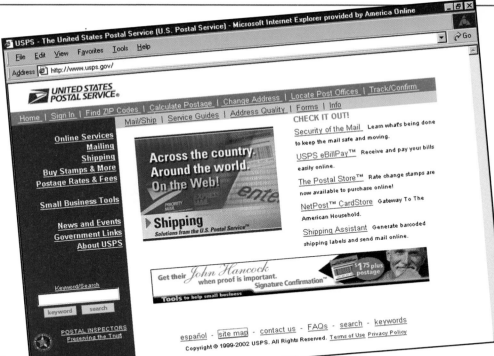

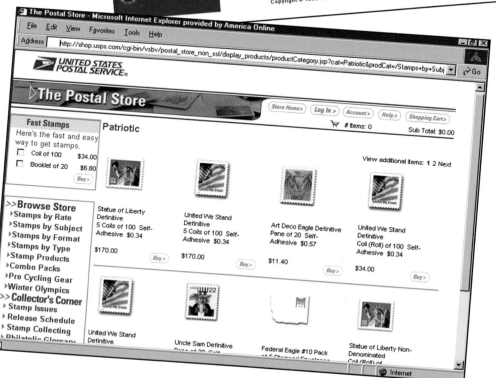

Chapter 6

Today's Mail: From ZIP Codes to E-Mail

In 1943, cities had become so big that the Post Office Department divided them into numbered zones. By 1963, the nation had grown so much that the Post Office began using Zoning Improvement Plan Codes, or ZIP Codes. Each area was given five numbers. The numbers became the last part of an address. ZIP Codes helped postal workers sort bundles of mail with sorting machines.

In 1970, Congress replaced the Post Office Department with the United States Postal Service. The postal service would still be

People can look up ZIP codes and buy stamps online (left).

owned by the federal government, but it would run as a more independent business.

In 1977, the Postal Service began Express Mail. Express Mail delivers letters and packages by the next day to certain areas around the country. The service costs more than other mail.

The 1980s saw many changes in the way people receive letters and other news.

Facsimile, or fax, machines were in more businesses and homes. Once big and heavy, they became smaller and not as costly.

Computers and fax machines may make communicating faster, but people still like to get mail.

Fax machines use electric signals from a telephone line to copy words or pictures. With the right telephone number, people can send letters and pictures by fax. It takes minutes for it to reach another fax machine anywhere in the world.

E-mail, or electronic mail, is a message sent from one computer to another over telephone lines. In 1971, Ray Tomlinson, an engineer, wrote the first electronic mail, or e-mail, program. He used the @ sign, which later became part of people's e-mail addresses. At the time, e-mail was only used in the computer industry.

In the 1990s, computers were made smaller and not as costly. With an electronic address, people could send and receive typed messages, any day and at any time.

By the year 2000, the Postal Service started using e-mail. A bill-paying system called USPS eBillPay lets people receive and pay bills electronically.

Yet even with new machines, Americans will always want to see what the letter carrier has brought them. People still want to receive and send mail.

A Native American tribe in Supai, Arizona, needs the United States Postal Service more than most people. The Havasupai tribe lives at the bottom of the Grand Canyon. Letter carriers deliver mail on

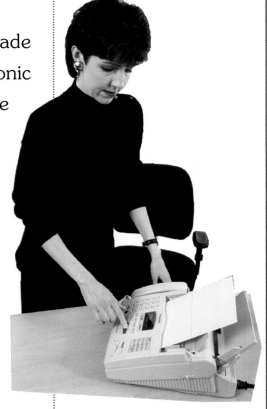

Fax machines use electric signals from a telephone line to copy words or pictures.

foot, mule, or horse. The only way in or out of Supai is by following an eight-mile trail. The U.S. Postal Service uses mules to deliver mail, food, and even furniture to the village. The animals make the three- to five-hour trip five days a week.

The Havasupai must have their mail. And they know it will come. The U.S. mail is a

Mules help deliver the mail to the Havasupai tribe in Supai, Arizona.

service everyone counts on—just as Benjamin Franklin hoped it would be years ago.

The United States Postal Service has helped shape America. It built the post roads in colonial times. It was there at the start of steamboat, railroad, airplane, and highway travel. It united the country as people moved west. And it has kept us united.

The mules bring the Havasupai everything from mail and food to furniture.

How to
Address an Envelope

Put your address here.

Put a stamp here.

Edgar Dog
1234 Street Ave.
Any Town, State 11111

Basil Cat
987 Boulevard
Any Place, State 99999

Put your family or friend's address here.

Timeline

1775—Benjamin Franklin is named Postmaster General at the Second Continental Congress.

1820—The Post Office Department uses steamboats to carry the mail.

1847—The first postal stamps are sold.

1860—The Pony Express begins.

1864—The first Railroad Post Office is set up.

1896—Rural Free Delivery begins in West Virginia.

1913—Parcel Post service starts for packages. It uses a Collect-on-Delivery (C.O.D.) plan to help people order things by mail.

1921—Airmail service begins from New York City to San Francisco.

1963—ZIP Codes are used to sort the mail faster.

1971—The United States Post Office Department becomes the United States Postal Service; Ray Tomlinson sends the first e-mail.

1977—Express Mail, an overnight service for letters and packages, begins.

1992—Stamps are sold through automatic machines.

2000—The Postal Store opens on the Internet.

Words to Know

buggy—A wagon that can seat at least one person and is pulled by a horse.

carrier—A post office worker who delivers or picks up mail.

colony—Land owned by the British that became part of the United States.

Congress—The part of the United States government that makes laws.

constitution—A plan of government that sets the laws of a state or nation.

engineer—A person who builds machines.

postage—The money needed to mail something.

route—The area a letter carrier delivers mail to.

stagecoach—A large carriage pulled by horses, with an outside seat in front for the driver.

tavern—A meeting place in colonial times.

trail—A path made by people or animals.

Learn More About
the U.S. Mail

Books

Brimner, Larry Dane. *E-Mail*. Danbury, Conn.: Children's Press, 2000.

Johnston, Marianne. *Let's Visit the Post Office*. New York: The Rosen Publishing Group, Inc., 1999.

Kroll-Smith, Steven. *Pony Express!* New York: Scholastic, 2000.

Internet Addresses

History of the United States Postal Service

<http://www.usps.gov/history/his1.htm>

This site from the United States Postal Service gives brief details about the history of the postal service.

Smithsonian National Postal Museum

<http://www.si.edu/postal/>

Click on "Games" or "Learn More About It" at this site from the Smithsonian Institution.

Index

A

Advanced Facer-Canceler
System, 14–15
airmail, 34–36
American Revolution, 25,
27

C

canceled stamps, 14, 16
colonial America, 21
Congress, 28, 36
Constitution, 27
Constitutional Post, 24

D

Delivery Bar Code
System, 17

E

e-mail, 40–41
Express Mail, 40

F

facsimile (fax) machine,
40
Fairbanks, Richard, 22
first-class mail, 37
Franklin, Benjamin,
23–25, 29, 43

G

Goddard, William, 24
Grand Canyon, 41

H

Hamilton, Andrew, 22
Haslam, Robert, 7, 9–10
Havasupai tribe, 41–43

K

King George III, 24

M

mail collection boxes,
13–14, 19, 29
Mail Recovery Centers,
18, 25
Multiline Optical
Character Reader, 15

N

Neale, Thomas, 22

O

Overland Mail Company,
11

P

Parcel Post, 33
Pony Express, 5–11
post, 21
Postmaster General, 22–25
post office, 14–19, 21,
27
Post Office Department,
27–29
post roads, 22–24, 43

R

railroad, 28, 30
Remote Bar Coding
System, 15–16
Rural Free Delivery,
33–34
Russell, William H., 5–6

S

Second Continental
Congress, 25
Special Delivery, 31
stagecoach, 5
stamps, 19, 28–29
steamboat, 28
Supai, Arizona, 41–42

T

telegraph, 10–11, 29

U

United States Postal
Service, 39

W

Washington, George W.,
26, 28–29
Western Union, 29
Wright, Orville, 34
Wright, Wilbur, 34

Z

ZIP Code, 15, 18, 39

48